AF367399

KOLIMA
BOOKS

Category: Leaders & Management

Original title: *Samurái, el que lidera sirviendo*
English edition: June 2021
First edition: February 2019
Second edition: September 2019
© 2021 Editorial Kolima, Madrid

Author: Enric Lladó Micheli
Translation: Araceli Guillamón
Editorial management: Marta Prieto Asirón
Cover phototypesetting: Sergio Santos Palmero
Book phototypesetting: Marta Fernández Zubeldia
Illustrations: Oriol Alcober

ISBN: 978-84-18811-04-3

*The master's teachings
are taken in through the eyes and the ears,
but they settle in the heart
and are passed down wordlessly
from one generation to the next.
This is the way the master
becomes immortal.*

*This book has been written
to honour all my masters.*

TABLE OF CONTENTS

FOREWORD

n 2014, a Japanese company assigned me a very interesting project.

The objective was to identify the most relevant skills that their executives needed in order to take on the challenges of the future.

The result was the creation of the Samurai Model, a beautiful analogy where I describe the four essential skills that will allow any person to both lead and stand out within an organisation, whilst bringing success to the organisation itself.

Since then, thousands of executives from the world's first-rate companies have been trained in the four arts of this model.

This book is a testimony of its essential philosophy. Firstly, as a way to support those students who have already begun to tread this path and are still evolving. Secondly, to assist those who wish to approach a very special way of understanding leadership; the kind of leadership of those who think personal success means working on the organisation's success.

The leadership of those who lead by serving.

*The master said that the invisible
may only be perceived
by conferring it different forms,
but it may only be learnt
by stripping it from all form.*

METAMORPHOSIS

t all starts again after the great fire of Hiroshima and Nagasaki.

The samurai had transformed themselves before. When they ceased to cut the air with the edge of their swords and began to cut it with the wings of their military airplanes.

After the Armageddon, eternal enemies took new forms and the battlefields shifted towards the hearts of corporations.

Then came the time to transmute old war weapons to other of a much more subtle kind.

For the *gaijin*[1], the samurai died centuries ago. Because the *gaijin* only perceive form. In their ignorance, they translate the word 'samurai' as 'warrior'. Still, a warrior (*bushi*) is not necessarily a samurai. Nor is the samurai necessarily a *bushi*.

Today less than ever.

---

1   *Gaijin*: foreigner.

THE ONE WHO SERVES

The samurai were, are, and always will be, those who serve others.

In the past, a samurai would serve an Army. Now they serve a corporation, a team or a family.

This is their true nature. The essence that transcends beyond any form. Serving a lord. A warrior without a lord is just a *ronin* wandering through the limbo and whose soul is getting dangerously close to the hell's abyss.

A lord may have many forms. But here too, form holds little importance. The lord is not a man or a woman. The lord is not a flag. The lord is not a corporation.

The lord is an idea for which it is worth dying, and beyond that, it is an idea for which it is worth living.

It has always been hard to know how to choose the right lord. Since ideas do not belong to this world, but inhabit another, more subtle place. And the only way of serving ideas is serving other people and organisations.

Making a mistake in choosing a person or an organisation is painful; making a mistake in choosing an idea, more so. But making mistakes is an essential part of the way of the samurai.

That is why it has always been better to serve the wrong lord than to serve none at all. Serving the wrong lord is not a sin. Serving more than expected is not a sin either. Those who really sin are those who serve no one but themselves.

After all, those who do not serve, serve no purpose at all.

Only those who serve humbly are those who truly lead.

That is why it is written that whoever is able to bow with pure honesty, will make the entire universe bow in return.

DECEIT

hose who serve no other but themselves hinder their business, thus hindering their own being too. They are deceiving themselves.

But those who wish to serve their organisation may also fall into deception. The cemetery is full of people who had good intentions and companies with ideas and talent.

Because in the company's body, what is good for the mouth may be bad for the liver. But the mouth does not know that.

Because sometimes the lizard must sacrifice its tail in order to save itself. But that is something that the tail cannot understand.

As Seneca said, 'senators are very intelligent but the Senate is completely stupid'. The samurai lead by serving and serve by leading, because they have outwitted this deception.

The samurai have reached mastery in the four arts. The four arts that are not taught in schools. The four arts that may be explained but can only be passed down wordlessly from *sensei*[2] to *seito*[3], incarnated in alive example.

Because these arts arise not from the knowledge but from the being.

And the being cannot deceive nor can be deceived.

---

2   *Sensei*: teacher.

3   *Seito*: student.

GREAT TRUTHS

A single man may survive on small truths, but a great company can only fulfill its purpose by reaching great truths.

Great truths are accessed through small truths, but not all small truths take you to a great truth.

The task of the samurai is to guide their company towards these great truths.

The tools of the samurai are the four arts.

The technique of the samurai emerges from their soul.

THE TECHNIQUE AND THE SOUL

The samurai's technique may be perceived in their words and actions.

The samurai's soul may be perceived in the way they speak and act.

The master warns:

Technique without soul is empty, useless and dangerous.

Soul without technique always leads towards technique.

Dark souls jeopardise their best gifts to develop their technique and put it at the service of their own darkness. They are a minority surrounded by a dark and foul halo. The greater their gifts, the bigger their fall.

Hazy souls lack strength. They walk in whatever direction and arrive nowhere. Their technique is a dim glint that disappears as quickly as it appeared. They are an odd minority, because without summing or subtracting, they end up multiplying.

Luminous souls give themselves away without expecting anything in return. They do not seek technique, but receive it; they do not long for recognition, but find it; they do not wish to stand out, but they are the most select minority.

They only wish to serve and that is why they lead.

Because those who lead are not the smartest, nor the strongest, nor the richest. Those may give orders, but giving orders is not leading.

The only ones who will lead will be those who really deserve it.

THE FOUR ARTS

The path to the great truth always starts with *Kyu Do*, the art of archery, which was transmuted into the art of making proposals.

A proposal is an arrow that points towards a truth. In combat, most of the arrows will be lost without hitting their target, but archers are always in the battlefront because their incessant arrows allow the detachments' progress.

But shooting arrows is not enough.

The great truth can only be accessed by those who dominate *Ai Ki Do*, the path of non-violent combat, the art of using the enemy's energy to defeat them, of winning softly without suffering any injuries nor provoking them.

Ai Ki Do was transmuted into the art of making powerful questions, the art of questioning instead of arguing. Using an argument to defend yourself from another argument is like using a fist to defend yourself from another fist. On the contrary, no fallacious argument can resist the force of a friendly question. Questions illuminate the path across the clouds of arrows.

Yoroi, the third art, is the art of the perfect armour. No one in their right mind would go into battle without an armour, but no one should protect themselves so much as to lose the speed of their movements. *Yoroi* becomes the art of making powerful decisions. Decisions that keep us protected yet at the same time make us lethal.

The fourth art is *Gunbai*, the art of the war fan, which is used to send signals to the troops but may also be used as a weapon to strike the opponent.

Gunbai's metamorphosis generates the art of fair criticism. Through criticism we receive information that is essential to learn, but criticism can also be very painful. Those who dominate *Gunbai*, the art of fair criticism, are capable of showing the toughest truths without inflicting any pain.

THE PATH

When a samurai makes a good proposal (*Kyu Do*), others dispute it with elevated questions (*Ai Ki Do*). In this process, the proposal either dies or is transformed and progresses.

Then comes the time of making powerful decisions, taking on risks and bringing the proposal into action (*Yoroi*).

Action is the judge that confronts theories with reality. Its blossom is the fruit of truth.

The fruit that stays on the ground will rot and disappear.

The samurai is responsible of picking up the fruit and offering it in the form of fair criticism (*Gunbai*). Sometimes the fruit is sweet, others is bitter.

Sweet or bitter, it always hides a great truth.

For that reason, those who ingest the fruit will be transformed. Because truth will grow within them.

It was written on fire that this is the only path to the great truth.

Those who are blind fail to see it, but get burnt nonetheless.

弓道

KYU DO

THE ART OF MAKING PROPOSALS

IMMORTAL SPIRIT

We pronounce '*Kyu Do*' and we are saying the way of the bow.

But all words are futile to describe this ancestral art.

The samurai have zealously protected their legacy throughout the centuries. That is why it survives intact to the arrival of firearms and the end of wars.

Those who practise the art – men, women, elders and children – gather together at the training fields in search of *mushin*, a mental state of profound emptiness.

From this state, the archer finally ceases to be the main obstacle in the path of the arrow and becomes an agent of fate.

Today, the spirit of *Kyu Do* transcends the physical dimension of the arch and manifests itself transmuted into the art of making proposals.

IMMORTAL SPIRIT

Good archers do not solve their problems by complaining. They shoot arrows instead. Good archers are always ready to shoot the first arrow. Good archers never run out of arrows.

Good samurai do the same with their proposals.

After all, by complaining the most you ever get is an apology, but by proposing the best thing you can get is exactly what you proposed.

Because in a conversation, the first to make a proposal is the one who decides the course the conversation will take.

Because in a negotiation, who makes more proposals is the one who gets the biggest slice of the cake.

Because in an argument, the proposal that is being discussed is the one that will have higher chances of succeeding.

For all these reasons, the one who makes proposals becomes the one who takes the lead.

STRENGTH

The ninety-nine-year-old man shot two arrows and both hit the target. The ten-year-old child hit the target once. The twenty-five-year-old man did not hit the target at all.

'But I'm stronger than both of you,' said the young man.

'It's not a matter of strength,' said the old man. 'The art of *Kyu Do* is only given to those who give themselves to it.'

You do not need to be more powerful, more intelligent, nor to occupy a high place in the hierarchy to make good proposals.

You just need to shoot many proposals and shoot them from the heart.

PREPARATION

It only takes an instant for the arrow to be shot. Preparing for that moment takes a whole lifetime.

A billion dollars proposal was made and accepted in a matter of minutes. That was all one could see.

Preparing that proposal took hundreds of hours. But no one saw that.

Gods bless the most gifted in their cribs. But at the battlefield, they only bless those who are best prepared.

For that reason, those who possess a well-prepared proposal may have hit their target long before they shot the arrow.

THE POSITION

The one who hits the target is not the one with the best aim, but the one standing closer to it.

The humblest of archers may inflict a fatal wound on the enemy's general just by standing at the right place.

Those who scorn the humblest arrow have not understood anything at all.

Great generals treasure with reverence the very last of the Army's thousands of arrows. Great business people receive with reverence every single one of their employees' proposals.

Because they know that all arrows and all proposals always point to some truth.

Great generals love every one of their soldiers equally and that is why they position them in different places. Great business people love all of their employees equally and that is why they give them different functions.

Because those who love their body, love every single one of the organs that compose it, regardless of their function.

POTENTIAL

hose who shoot their arrows from the top of the hill reach twice as far with double the force and will destroy their enemies.

Those who shoot from the deepest end of the valley do not reach very far, and will lose their arrows among the bushes.

The only battle that a general fights in the deepest end of the valley takes place when he has been ambushed. Usually, he will lose it, but the real defeat took place before the battle even started.

For that reason, general *Sun Tzu* claimed that most battles are won long before they get started.

Those who make a proposal from the wrong place and at the wrong time have lost the battle before it has started. The proposal will be lost forever among the brambles of a 'no'.

The art of *Kyu Do* without strategy, is not *Kyu Do*. Good strategists are patient and wait calm until they find the right time and place.

That is how they manage to harness the proposal's full potential.

THE TARGET

hose who are thinking of hitting the target will fail.

Those who keep their mind empty in every tiny gesture and simply follow each step correctly, cannot prevent the arrow from meeting the target.

Likewise, those who are thinking of getting their proposal accepted will fail.

Those who are free of their ego in every step they take, from the very moment they start preparing the proposal to the very moment the last word leaves their mouths, will inevitably trigger the beginning of a change.

CHANGE

An inflexible arrow will trace a devious path.

An arrow that bends and spins on itself travels in a straight line.

Short and devious is the journey of a proposal that does not allow to be transformed.

Good samurai wish for their proposal to be altered by others because they know that each time this happens, the arrow changes for the better and gains more and more speed.

They know that change is only induced by change.

So those who want to change something, must change themselves first.

Those who love their arrows as much as they love themselves will shoot none trying to keep them intact.

They will die with their arrows in their hands and the enemy's in their hearts.

ONE IN TEN

In the training field heaven, one in every two arrows hits the target.

In the battlefield hell, one in every ten arrows will hit the target.

Those who scorn the nine missed arrows, do not understand the laws of combat.

Because when everything is still, the arrows are meant to hit the target.

But when everything is in movement, five are used to discover where not to aim, four to stop the enemy's advance and only one in ten is meant to hit the target.

But the tenth arrow can only succeed once the other arrows have fulfilled their purpose.

Those who grow desperate and give up after the ninth proposal have been defeated because they do not understand the rules of business.

合気道

AI KI DO

THE ART OF ASKING QUESTIONS

O'SENSEI

In the year 1960, Morihei Ueshiba was decorated by emperor Hiroito. This act constituted the public recognition for a lifetime dedicated to the search of peace. A search that took place amidst the violence and barbarity of the wars in which he found himself involved.

A search that culminated in 1942, when O'Sensei lived his third and last experience of spiritual awakening, which he called '*The Great Spirit of Peace*'. A celestial ray of light gave birth to *Ai Ki Do*, the supreme martial art, created to transcend the violence of this world once and for all.

Today it counts with thousands of followers and with them the spirit of O'Sensei has transcended the limits of the *dojo*[4] and the nations.

Transmuted into the art of asking questions, it turns its carrier into an agent of peace, change and progress.

---

4   *Dojo*: place where martial arts are practiced. Literally, the place where the path lies.

SYMMETRY

A common person is a monkey fighting against its own reflection.

The samurai are those who have seen the mirror.

They search inside for what is necessary outside.

By changing themselves, they transform the entire world.

For that reason, the path of *Ai Ki Do* always starts within oneself and only those who start by serving will be the ones who will finally lead.

RESISTANCE

Every action has a reaction.

This is why in combat, those who push another are pushing themselves, and those who resist a thrust are lending it strength.

Likewise, those who deny a name, are remembering it; those who resist an idea, are making it stronger; those who criticise a proposal, are bringing it to life and those who intend to take control, have just given it away.

That is why *Ai Ki Do* practitioners do not resist but flow, do not confront but unite, they are not lineal, but circular.

They do not argue, but question.

THE WEIGHT OF TRUTH

In the face of an attack, *Ai Ki Do* practitioners use the force of gravity to redirect their opponents' weight against themselves. The larger the opponents, the greater their fall.

In the face of a proposal, samurai use the weight of truth to redirect the proposal against itself, simply by asking questions.

If the proposal is weak, the weight of truth will make it collapse.

If it stands, accepting it will be a divine gift.

Those who master the technique of *Ai Ki Do* will stand unalterable before any opponent, whatever their size. And those who know the weight of truth, will stand unalterable before any unfavourable proposal, whatever its importance.

BEING RIGHT

A number is painted on the ground.

The person looking at it from above says it is a six. The person looking at it from below says it is a nine.

Who is right?

Students of truth say both are right, but the master of truth says both are right yet at the same time neither is.

As long as they think that the other is wrong, neither is right.

Those who deeply understand this may become free of the weight of their ego. Only then will they be able to apply the full weight of truth.

SILENCE

The first step before asking is listening. The only way to listen is to remain silent.

But the silence of sown lips is not real silence. That was Gandhi's lesson. True silence is practised with our mouth, face, hands, body, mind, emotion and ego.

True silence is a profound emptiness of pure receptivity.

For that reason, samurai are silent and empty individuals. Their emptiness exerts a captivating force of attraction. Since they listen to everyone, everyone listens to them.

Therefore, those who speak and speak without end are following, while those who remain silent are actually leading.

THE APPLE

The lord asked his servants to bring him an apple each. One brought a red apple, another brought a green apple and the last one brought a yellow one.

Who had understood him?

All and none.

People believe that they understand each other, but the truth is that they only understand a small part. This is dangerous.

Because those who misinterpret an attack will respond with useless technique.

Those who wish to serve well repeat what they have heard to make sure they have understood. This is the second step before asking.

If they misunderstood, now they will understand correctly. If they did understand, the other will feel understood. And those who feel understood will then wish to understand in return.

Therefore, those who make an effort to understand the other seem to be following but are actually leading.

VALUE

ho underestimates the enemy's blows will end up defeated. For even the little finger of a child, when aimed at the eye's centre, is enough to defeat a giant.

An *Ai Ki Do* practitioner values every single attack and therefore can manage them all in the right measure.

Likewise, who does not value an unfavourable proposal becomes more vulnerable to it.

The samurai values every proposal and shows appreciation to the person that made it, especially when the proposal can damage the samurai interests. This is the third step before asking questions.

Lao Tsé said that those who wish to get something from someone must give something first. Thus, who wish to be valued must value the other first.

Very few value the other first, because very few have the necessary valour.

It so happens that those who value others and are truly thankful seem to be serving, but are really leading and no proposal will ever hurt them.

IRIMI

When someone tries to hit us, we step back to avoid the impact because we are scared of getting hurt.

Those who practise *Ai Ki Do* do not step back. Instead, they do *Irimi* (entering) seeking to make full contact and reaching a complete union. Once both bodies become one, they can start redirecting the movement.

Those who listen to a proposal first, then repeat it to make sure that they have understood, and finally show their gratitude in a sincere way, get into full contact with the proposal and become connected to the other. They are doing *Irimi*. Now they may begin to ask questions.

Those who do not listen, nor reformulate, nor show any gratitude, do not make any advance but go backwards because they fear to be convinced by the other. Their ego is scared of being hurt.

Perhaps they believe that they are leading, but are following instead.

MUSIC

The spirit of *Ai Ki Do* is not to hurt the attacker but to neutralise the attack.

The spirit of questioning is not to hurt the person who is being questioned but to discover their truth.

Hurtful questions can never be good questions. They are perceived as a masked attack. Far from pacifying, they cause even more stir and contribute to the escalation of conflict. They are worse than a direct attack.

It is not the lyrics that causes the damage but the music with which the question is asked. Because lyrics show our doubts on the subject, but music reveals what we think of the other person.

Those who ask to hurt believe that the other is undesirable. Those who ask to subdue believe that the other is inferior. Those who ask to manipulate believe that the other is stupid. And for these reasons they will be resisted.

Those who ask to understand believe that the other is reasonable. Those who ask to learn believe that the other is wise. Those who ask to serve believe that the other is worthy. And for these reasons they are followed in the path towards truth.

Truth is never reached by those who wish to win, nor by those who wish to convince. Only by those who seek it amicably.

大鎧

YOROI

THE ART OF
MAKING DECISIONS

SKIN

he *gaijin* see *Yoroi*[5] as nothing else than a lifeless object.

Yet *Yoroi* is real skin that has been regenerating itself from the beginning of times with the only purpose of serving the one who serves.

Generation after generation it has stayed true to one fundamental principle: agility over safety.

This principle expresses in leather and metal the true nature of the samurai's soul.

Today, those who lead their businesses with the courage of their decisions, whether wearing heels or a suit, keep this spirit intact upon their skin.

---

5   *Yoroi*: samurai armor.

SAFETY

Making decisions is like going into combat.

Those who do not wear enough protection will die.

Those who protect themselves in excess will not advance and will end up defeated. Because in the search for absolute safety, they are putting themselves at risk.

This is why the cemetery is full of valiants but it is also full of cowards. Even though cowards lived an hour longer, that hour was worthless.

A good armour is the one that protects while allowing freedom of movement. It is designed to both protect the wearer and to allow him to attack.

A good decision is both reasonable and intrepid. Its function is to safeguard our own estate at the same time as we conquer the enemy's.

THE VOICE OF DEATH

Those who never go into combat keep their armour intact. The armour of a true warrior is full of dents and scratches.

The sound of each impact is the voice of death calling at the door. It reminds the warrior that although he is protected, he is still vulnerable. It produces a bittersweet feeling.

Those who make decisions receive impacts in their businesses. The sound of the blows is the voice of failure calling at their door. It reminds them of their vulnerability as much as it reminds them they are protected. It is a bittersweet feeling.

Those who do not perceive that bittersweet taste on their palates are not making decisions nor are going into combat. This is dangerous.

Because by trying to stay away from combat to avoid death they end up stuck in a bog where death will finally find them.

THE GOOD DECISION

What is the difference between a good and a bad decision?

'That only the good decision will get the expected results,' say the students.

'That could be a way of differentiating them, but by then you would already be dead,' replies the master.

Anyone can criticise a general's decision once the battle has ended. Few do so at the moment the decision is being made.

'A good decision is not measured by its outcome but by the way it was made', the master said.

Those who follow thoroughly the right steps to make a decision always take the right decision.

Ultimately, it is fate who decides. But whatever the outcome, the samurai keep their honour intact because they have done the right thing.

BALANCE

The three main steps to wearing an armour are adjusting the *kabuto*[6] to protect the head, securing the *do*[7] to protect the heart, and attaching the *haidate*[8] to protect the legs. If any of these elements fails, the armour will not be safe and the warrior will be in danger.

A good decision requires using one's mind to be reasonable, one's heart to channel emotions, and one's legs to move quickly into action.

Making decisions without reason is what fools do. Making decisions without emotions is what the corrupt do. Making decisions without movement is what the useless do.

All of them will end up being victims of their lack of balance.

---

6   *Kabuto*: helmet.

7   *Do*: breastplate.

8   *Haidate*: thighs armor.

KABUTO

he master asks what the half of two plus two is.

The students answer two.

The master replies three.

Those who do not know how to make decisions believe that their problem is the lack of information. But the real problem is that they are not able to read the information they already have.

They are their own enemies and become victims of the *yurei*[9] inhabiting their minds.

Those who believe that their mind do not have *yurei* are the first to succumb to them.

---

9   *Yurei*: ghost. Literally, a diffuse spirit.

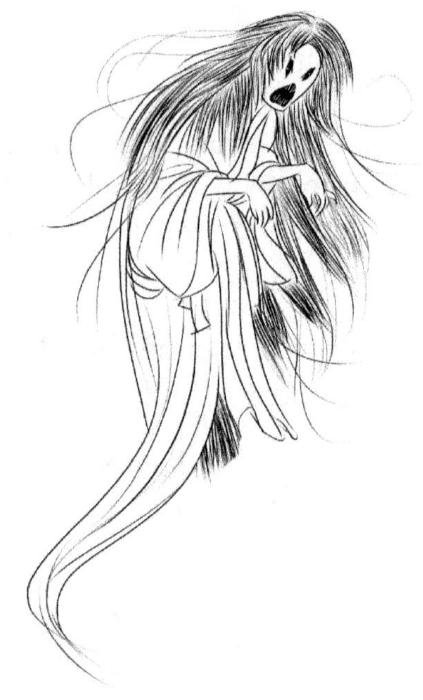

YUREI

The child shouts scared that there is a *yurei* in his wardrobe. His father comes into the room, turns on the light, opens the wardrobe and shows the child that there is nothing there other than the shadows of his mind. Then the child falls calmly asleep.

Those who have *yurei* in their minds and do not confront them out of fear or laziness, are feeding them. These ghosts will slowly grow until the person is consumed by darkness. The presence of yurei reflects the absence of yoroi.

There are countless *yurei* invading the minds and seeking to conquer the world to fill it with shadows.

But no *yurei* can survive the light of a bright question. They vanish into space and their carrier is finally liberated and left in peace.

DO

At the battlefield, a mediocre but well executed decision is always better than a brilliant but poorly executed one.

If no one else takes part in the process of deciding, there will be no feeling of commitment and the decision will not be executed from the heart. Defeat is the only possible outcome.

Still, if too many people get involved, they will never reach a decision. This will also lead to disaster.

For that reason, generals involve those, and only those, who are indispensable to execute the decision on the battlefield, as well as those, and only those, who could prevent its execution.

THE RIGHT MEASURE

The general explains his decisions and his reasoning to armorers, cooks, servants and quartermasters, so that they may carry out their task from their hearts. This is the most subtle level of involvement.

Those soldiers who risk their lives in the battlefield are granted voice in the decision-making process. By listening to them with honest consideration, the general frees their hearts so that they might give everything in the battlefield, no matter what the final decision may be.

The regiments' captains are granted voice and agency. Their hearts become one with the decision and their determination will remain strong, if necessary, until the annihilation of the last of their men.

Finally, the general gives his lord absolute power to decide over him. He involves everyone else with his example, sacrificing his own life if necessary.

HAIDATE

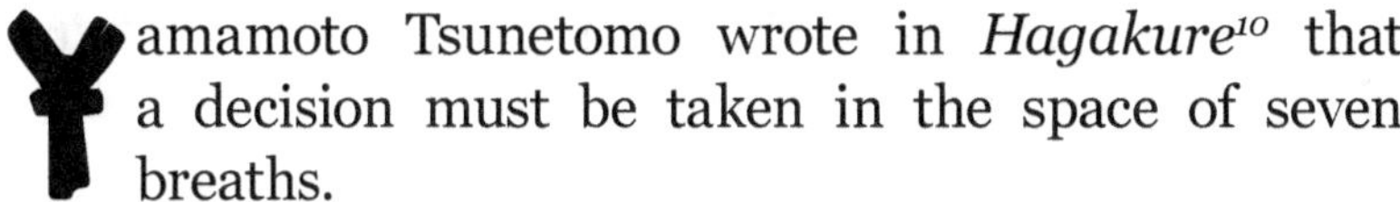

amamoto Tsunetomo wrote in *Hagakure*[10] that a decision must be taken in the space of seven breaths.

Less than seven would be too rushed and more than seven would be too idle. Exactly seven is perfection.

Those who decide how to decide while they are deciding, take seven thousand breaths.

Those who are unclear about when to decide, decide in the last minute and thus decide poorly.

Those who know when they must begin and end deciding, as well as the steps they must follow in between, know the value of agility and time becomes their ally.

---

10   *Hagakure*: 'Hidden by the Leaves', written version of the *bushido*, the warrior's code.

ELEVEN CURSES

Cursed are those who want to have it all, because they will never achieve a thing.

Cursed are those affraid to clear their ideas, because they will disappear into shadows.

Cursed are those who do not make decisions, because their enemies will decide for them.

Cursed are those who talk but do not act, because death will find them waiting.

Cursed are those who act with doubts, because they are committing suicide.

Cursed are those who act without thinking, because they drag their people to their graves with them.

Cursed are those who do not act conscientiously, because they have just become corrupted.

Cursed are those who act without heart, because they will be left alone in the face of danger.

Cursed are those who desire to please everyone, because they will satisfy no one.

Cursed are those who do not respond with their own lives, because they risk those of their own people.

Cursed are those who never go first, because they will always fall behind.

軍配

GUNBAI

THE ART OF FAIR CRITICISM

TESSENJITSU

hen samurai were forbidden to enter public spaces armed, they transformed their fans into combat weapons. Conferring them a deadly core of steel, they created *tessenjitsu*, the refined art of fighting with fans.

Gunbai, the solid fan, was born in this technological path. With its curious butterfly shape, it is used to send signals to the troops in the battlefield at the same time it serves its carrier as a powerful defence and attack weapon.

Today the *gunbai* stays alive in the sumo *dojo*, where the *gyoji*[11] wields it to give instructions to the contenders and to declare the winner at the end of the match.

The art of good criticism is *gunbai* because it homes the same spirit and is ruled by the same principles.

---

11   *Gyoji*: sumo referee.

INTENTION

Why do the incautious speak?
Because they cannot keep their mouths shut.

Why do the resentful speak?
Because they are thirsty of revenge.

Why do the perverse speak?
Because they are cheating someone.

Why do the samurai speak?
Because it is their responsibility.

BLINDNESS

The master challenged the students: 'Tell me how many freckles you have without looking at yourself in the mirror'. The students looked at each other puzzled.

Finally, one asked another to count his freckles.

No one is capable of looking in their own eyes. No one hears their own voice as they speak. No one can experience the taste of their own tongue. No one can bite their own teeth.

The blind spot of the observer is always the observer himself.

Because we cannot see ourselves. And sometimes we do not really want to do so.

Those who wish to see themselves will always need the help of others.

For that reason, those who humbly help others to recognise their own truth are fulfilling their duty.

It looks like they are leading because they are honourably serving.

TWO-FACED

The general observed the movement of the troops from the mountain top and directed them with the *gunbai*. When two enemy soldiers reached the summit, the general used it to strike their heads open.

The unknown truth is like a *gunbai*, because it is always two-faced. It can nurture or can get stuck in one's throat, it can guide or disorient, it can motivate or discourage.

Those who use their truth to help others, lead the company to success. They are samurai.

Those who employ their truth to damage and punish others, live in shadows, deceit and pain. They are *ninja*.

Those who intend the former but achieve the latter do not understand what they really have in their hands.

PORCELAIN

A stumble threw the vase on the floor where it shattered into pieces. They managed to rebuild it with patience, but it was never the same again.

The heart's flesh is fine porcelain. The slightest nudge will break it and then the relationship will never be the same again.

Improperly wielded criticism strikes as hard as a *gunbai* in one's face. It destroys the relationship and has no way back.

Skilfully wielded criticism is as soft as the breeze of a faraway *gunbai*. It is often useless, but always leaves open the possibility to try again.

SWEET FRUIT

When the fruit of truth is sweet, the samurai offer it in abundance.

No one asked for it, that is why they are leading.

No one expects it, but everyone receive it with pleasure.

This is how they bring joy to everyone's palates and prepare them for the time when different flavoured fruits ripen.

Those who only give away the bitter fruit of criticism when their own interests have been compromised are simply reacting, and for that reason they are not leading but following, they do not please and are not followed.

BITTER FRUIT

When the fruit of truth is bitter, the samurai wait for it to be requested before giving it away.

If no one requests it, then they wait for the right time and place. They prepare it conveniently and only offer it to those who are capable of swallowing it and whenever they are ready.

After all, when the art of criticism lacks strategy, it is just the same as gambling.

The court's buffoon can mock the monarch without fear of losing his head because he has already asked the king's forgiveness for what he is about to say. Only if the monarch accepts, will the buffoon proceed.

The samurai may say whatever they like to whoever they like because they wait for the right time and place, they know the right procedure and always arrive prepared.

USELESS PAIN

A father told his son that he was lazy. The son continued being lazy the rest of his life and carried a grudge in his heart.

Because criticising the other's identity causes a lot of pain and gives very little information. By trying to transform so much, one accomplishes very little.

The father told another son that he was unable to make his bed properly. The son reluctantly changed some things but was still too far from his father's suggestions.

Because criticising someone's ability is also hurtful, and thought it gives away more information, it is insufficient.

The father told his third son that whenever he left his sheets creased and his pillow out of place, his mother had to unmade the bed completely and made it all over again. This son made the effort to leave his bed neat and his pillow in place.

Because criticising behaviours gives away a lot more information and is often painless. For that reason, it is the only useful kind of criticism. It reaches far beyond than it seems.

ARGUMENT

Smoke signals are diffuse, imprecise and run the risk of being changed by the wind. Their interpretation is subject to discussion. That is why their use is limited and often problematic.

The signals of the *gunbai* are clear and specific. They leave no room for interpretation, preventing any possible arguments. *Gunbai* signals can guide an entire army.

Those who are generic in their criticism or leave room for interpretation are casting smoke signals and will end up tangled up in an argument. Because the sort of criticism that can be argued about will always be argued. And the very moment the argument begins, all criticism becomes completely sterile. When this happens, it is far better to retreat.

Contrarily, the samurai use the art of *gunbai* to describe behaviours and consequences in a very specific and detailed manner. Because they only wish to reflect facts and thus avoid any form of judgement or interpretation.

No one argues with them because there is nothing to argue about.

ACCEPTANCE

Who receives indisputable criticism often tries to justify his actions. It means that this criticism has not been completely accepted.

Then the samurai honestly accepts this justification and this is how his criticism is finally accepted.

Because who seeks acceptance must be the first to accept.

All the samurai's criticism is accepted because the samurai accepts all justifications as well as all criticism first.

The samurai is always the first to accept because in order to lead it is necessary to go first.

HARAKIRI[12]

Who has no choice but to accept criticism may feel a desire to do *harakiri* and immolate himself in front of the critic.

Allowing this to happen is cruel. It is not part of the art of *gunbai* but a product of the vice of revenge.

Good samurai possess good reflexes and are quick at interrupting the other with gratitude, praise and distractions at the slightest hint of acceptance.

Because the samurai are able to feel and anticipate the pain and heal it almost before it has even appeared.

Serving the other as humble support make the other progress. For that reason, when they serve, they are actually leading.

---

12   *Harakiri*: to pierce your stomach with your own sword.

It is now written that only those who serve will lead, and that those who lead only do so because they are serving.

Bright is the path of those who lead by serving, but it is also long and full of obstacles.

In this path, those who become friends of comfort will have a similar experience to the person who invited a burglar to dinner to their home.

Those who seek an easier path always end up going downhill.

Those who seek perfection will never achieve anything. Because perfection is a synonym of death.

Those who only seek to learn, take a step forward every day. Because learning is a synonym of life.

Those who rush their steps stumble. They soon become tired and never really get anywhere.

Those who walk slowly and steadily are the quickest to advance. Because patience, discipline and the repetition of *kata*[13] are the best allies of learning.

---

13   *Kata*: form.

Those who start their journey declaring war to the world, will always end up defeated. Because they are trying to bite a *katana*[14].

Those who accept reality without judging and are simply themselves, will never be defeated. Because the best fight is the one that never takes place, and the true enemy is always oneself.

Those who fear losing their live along the path, become a walking dead.

Those who become friends with death, will be the only ones to savour life.

And at the end of the journey, those who sought glory will not find it and those who find it will do so precisely because they were not searching for it.

---

14   *Katana*: sword.

KOLIMA
BOOKS